BRODY THE PIT BULL

written by: **Jeanine Saint Clare**

illustrated by: **Shane Whatley**

This book is dedicated to my dog Brody! Rescuing an animal is one of the greatest things you can do. You are saving a life! Those who say money cannot buy happiness, have never paid an adoption fee. I may have rescued Brody, but I can assure you that he's the one who rescued me! Love you Bubba!!!

Brody is a pit bull.

So people think
he's mean.

But Brody is the sweetest doggie
that you had ever seen.

Sometimes people see Brody
and will walk across the street.

I promise he's the friendliest
dog you will ever get to meet.

The dog park is one of
Brody's favorite places.

He runs around
with the other dogs
and jumps on
the people to kiss
their faces.

Brody is a silly dog
and his butt sure
can wiggle.

If you ever seen the
way he shakes it,
you would
start to giggle.

Once in a while
Brody goes in circles.
trying to catch his tail.

Brody always
lets me know
when we receive
the mail.

Brody loves to run
and pull me on my skates.

Brody even helps with the dishes by licking all the plates.

In the winter when it's cold
Brody loves his coat.

But in the summer he loves
the beach or being on a boat.

Brody absolutely loves to go
for rides in the car.

No matter where the adventure is,
if it's near or if it's far.

Brody used to live in the shelter.
It was such a crowded place.

Overflowing with so many dogs
who all shared the same sad face.

The shelter is a scary place.
It's loud, it's cold, and the
dogs are all alone.

Dreaming that someone
out there would just come
and take them all home.

Some rescues find foster homes
for all the doggies in need.

Opening your home
to a homeless dog makes
you an angel indeed!

The best thing I ever did
was go to the shelter
and set him free!

Brody is more than just a dog, he's my family!

The End

Made in the USA
Middletown, DE
27 February 2019